MW01288752

WALKING BY FAITH
— AND —
NOT BY SIGHT

TRUSTING GOD
WHEN LIFE DOES NOT MAKE SENSE

CHRISTIAN MARTIN

WESTBOW
P R E S S
A DIVISION OF THOMAS NELSON

WestBow Press books may be ordered through booksellers or by contacting:

WestBow Press
A Division of Thomas Nelson
1663 Liberty Drive
Bloomington, IN 47403
www.westbowpress.com
1-(866) 928-1240

Because of the dynamic nature of the Internet, any web addresses or links contained in this book may have changed since publication and may no longer be valid. The views expressed in this work are solely those of the author and do not necessarily reflect the views of the publisher, and the publisher hereby disclaims any responsibility for them.

Any people depicted in stock imagery provided by Thinkstock are models, and such images are being used for illustrative purposes only.

Certain stock imagery © Thinkstock.

ISBN: 978-1-4497-4504-2 (e)
ISBN: 978-1-4497-4505-9 (sc)

Library of Congress Control Number: 2012905907

Printed in the United States of America

WestBow Press rev. date: 05/03/2012

Contents

ACKNOWLEDGMENTS

The title of the book is credited to my mentor and friend, Michele Aikens. She was inspired by God to give me the title *Walking by Faith and Not by Sight: Trusting God when Life Does Not Make Sense* as my final writing assignment for ministry training. Thank you for acknowledging and validating my assignment.

I am very blessed to have had the opportunity to receive ministry training under the great leadership of my father in the ministry, Apostle H. Daniel Wilson, and Pastor Beverly L. Wilson. Thank you for training me to be an ambassador for the kingdom of God.

A special thank you to my family and friends who continue to support me, even when you don't understand the direction that God is taking me. Thank you for walking by faith with me. You enrich the quality of my life.

Mommy, thank you for encouraging me to spread my wings. You make me feel like there are no limits; I can do as much as I want to do and go as far as I want to go. Thank you for naming me Christian and for your sacrifice of giving me to God.

Dad, thank you for believing in me and supporting all of my endeavors.

I have the best grandmothers in the world! The love, support, and prayers of my grandmothers encourage me.

Aunt Alice, thank you for starting me on this journey of walking by faith. You taught me how to serve God faithfully in tithing, prayer, and studying the Word of God.

To my great son, Kevin, you are my first ministry. It is an awesome assignment to be your first mentor in business and ministry. Thank you for taking this journey of faith with me. May you glean from these experiences of faith great wisdom and insight into the power of God. Mommy loves you!

INTRODUCTION

Everyone will experience seasons of affliction—the grief of adversity, sickness, catastrophe, tragedy, or loss. When life cannot be summed up in practical intelligence, when we cannot make sense of our circumstance, we must walk by faith. To walk by faith is to move at a moderate (consistent and temperate) pace and conduct ourselves in a manner that coincides with what we believe, with the assurance (the confirmation) of the things that we hope for—perceiving them as real fact. We must perceive as real fact what is not yet revealed to our senses (what we cannot see), and we must not conduct ourselves according to our range of vision, because our vision is limited.[1]

Vision refers to one's ability to see; one's range of foresight; one's ability to believe. We must believe the promises of God. *You must be a visionary!* There will be times in your life when you will not understand your circumstances. You might find yourself baffled by the state of your affairs. During these times, you will have to rely on the vision of God.

The prophet Habakkuk wrestled with God on behalf of his people because he did not understand why God allowed wickedness to surround them. The Israelites were being overtaken by their enemy, the Chaldeans. The Chaldeans (Babylonians) were powerful and violent. God allowed them to take land that did not belong to them. God raised up a heathen nation for the purpose of punishing his own people. *Life did not make sense.* The chosen people of God were being destroyed by wickedness—with God's permission. Habakkuk questioned God—how long would he sit back and do nothing while his people suffered? They had become exhausted, depressed, and disappointed. God's response to the prophet was this: "Write *the vision*, and make it plain upon tables, that he may run that readeth it. For the vision is yet for an appointed time, but at the end *it* shall speak and not lie, though it tarry, wait for it; because it will surely come, it will not tarry . . . the just shall live by faith" (Habakkuk 2:2-4 KJV, emphasis added). God instructed the prophet Habakkuk to write the revelation—the vision. Your ability to see the vision of God during times of confusion, uncertainty, and chaos is paramount in your walk of faith. "Without faith it is impossible to please [God]" (Hebrews 11:6 KJV).

You must know that God knows your circumstances. He knows all of the situations that surround you and concern you. God is omniscient; he knows everything. God allowed your circumstances and he has made an appointment for your deliverance, a set time. The vision that God has given you shall speak and not lie.

I can recall a time when my life did not make sense. Several years ago, I was bewildered when it seemed that I had lost everything, all at once. After six years of marriage, my husband announced that he wanted a divorce. I was about six weeks pregnant with our son when he moved out and never looked back. My shock and embarrassment at his decision was coupled with joy and excitement about the baby. It was both the best and worst time of my life. When the divorce was finalized, I felt like God had allowed the enemy (Satan) to have victory over us. I wondered how two people who professed to have a relationship with God could not make a covenant relationship work. But that is another book!

Less than a year after the divorce, my baby and I were sleeping in our apartment when I was awakened by someone pounding on the door and screaming, "Get out, the building is on fire." It was a devastating fire in which we lost everything and nearly lost our lives. When we made it outside of the building, I turned around, looked up, and literally saw a big ball of fire rolling through the building. Some people were hanging out of windows screaming; others were jumping out of windows. It was a most horrific experience; the memories haunted me for nearly two years. Ten days after the fire, as I was attempting to pull my life together, a lady lost control of her car and hit my car with my baby and me inside, totaling both cars. I was convinced that the devil was trying to kill me. My life did not make sense!

I had a real relationship with God. I prayed every day, studied the word of God, and was an active member of my church. Yet I had to ask God, "Are you going to let the devil kill me?" God's immediate response was, "You're still alive." I knew at that moment that Satan could not kill me and that as long as I am alive there is hope. However, that hope quickly turned to fear. In one year, my life had been turned upside down. I had lost everything, and I did not understand why God had allowed these things to happen. Then the devil came after what was left—my mind. The catastrophic events, coupled with my dismay about why God would allow these circumstances, led to symptoms of posttraumatic stress disorder. The sound of sirens and the sight of flashing lights unnerved me. Paranoia, flashbacks, and the inability to sleep exhausted me. I lived in fear of what could happen next.

During this time, I never stopped praying and believing that God was still in control of my life. Periodically, I recalled visions and promises that God had given to me. However, I did not understand how my circumstances could work together for my good or lead to those promises of God. My life did not make sense, but I never walked away from God. I continued to walk by faith, knowing that the same God who had a plan to deliver Israel from Babylonian captivity had a plan to deliver me. God spoke through the prophet Jeremiah in Jeremiah 29:11 (KJV): "For I know the thoughts that I think toward you, saith the Lord, thoughts of peace, and not of evil, to give you an expected end." I believed that God had a plan! I relied on the word of God. I learned to eat the Word day and night. To eat the Word means to meditate on it, reflect on it, ingest it, and digest it. I metabolized the nutrients of the Word so that I would be sustained by it. Like food is converted into energy in our bodies, when I internalized the Word, I gained strength and courage. The Word of God was my solace, my source of comfort from emotional distress, sadness, and grief. I had faith that the word of God is true, and as my faith increased, so did my peace.

Examine the word *faith*. According to Hebrews 11:1 (AMP), "faith is the assurance (the confirmation, the title deed) of things [we] hope for, being the proof of things [we] do not see and the conviction of their reality; faith is perceiving as real fact what is not revealed to the senses." When someone has a title to a house or automobile, that title shows proof of ownership. Your faith in the word of God (the promises written in the Word of God and those that he has spoken directly to you based on his word), is the proof that you believe. It proves that the promises are yours. Your faith breathes life into the promises. As the promises of God are activated by your faith, you will be revitalized, encouraged, and stimulated. You will feel new life being breathed into you by the stirring of your faith. You will walk through life with peace and confidence in God. This confidence comes from being conscious of the power of God and relying on his power and not your own. "In the world, you have tribulation and trials and distress and frustration; but be of good cheer [take courage; be confident, certain, undaunted]! For I have overcome the world [I have deprived it of power to harm you and have conquered it for you]" (John 16:33 AMP).

Paul, in 2 Corinthians 5:7 (AMP), teaches the walk of faith like this: "We walk by faith [we regulate our lives and conduct ourselves by our conviction or belief respecting man's relationship to God and divine things, with trust and holy fervor; thus we walk] not by sight or appearance." Whatever God has promised you—*act like you already have it!* Walk according to the promise, not according to how you feel or according to your circumstances. Live cautiously with restraint and do not move hastily, or do anything that is contrary to the promise of God.

As I learned to walk by faith, I had to stop rehearsing my circumstances and begin to conduct myself in support of my belief in the promises of God. I took control of my thoughts and focused on the promises of God. This zeal led to a commitment, and soon a passion for the purpose of God emerged within me. Every word that God speaks is sacred; we must walk cautiously according to his word.

CHAPTER 1

TRUSTING GOD WHEN LIFE DOES NOT MAKE SENSE

During my times of trouble, disappointment, sadness, and grief, I learned that God is a protector and that he is trustworthy. God will hide you; he will shelter you in his secret place when you are in trouble.[1]

Who are *you*? You are not your job, your spouse, your home, your car, or your children. *You* are your hope, your faith, and your trust in God; this is who God will protect. God will fortify your hope, your faith, and your trust in Him. It is important to know this because you may lose your job, your spouse, your home, your car, or your children. However, you do not have to lose your hope, your faith, or trust in God.

Learning to trust God is a process that most often occurs during times of trial, trouble, or discontentment. It is very easy to say "I have faith" or "I trust God," when you have visible and tangible evidence that all is well. However, consider times of homelessness, abandonment, rejection, joblessness, sickness, divorce, barrenness, or difficulties with your children. Such circumstances test your spiritual development and trust in God. Each time you encounter tribulation, it is an opportunity for God to demonstrate his power. It is also an opportunity for you to demonstrate your reliance on God. Trust in God is established through experience with Him.

Trust is defined as firm reliance on the integrity, ability, or character of a person or thing.[2] Our ability to trust God rests on our confidence in and reliance on his character. The names of God describe his qualities and characteristics and substantiate that he is trustworthy. Let's examine God's qualities and characteristics.

NAMES/TITLES OF GOD	CHARACTERISTICS
ROCK	*God our Rock* Deuteronomy 32:18; 2 Samuel 23:3; 1 Corinthians 10:4
PRINCE OF PEACE	*Governor of Peace, Keeper of Peace, Commander of Peace* Isaiah 9:6
JEHOVAH-ROPHE	*Healer* Exodus 15:22-26; Jeremiah 17:14; Jeremiah 30:17; Matthew 8:7
JEHOVAH-JIREH	*Provider* Genesis 22:14; Deuteronomy 8:16
JEHOVAH-SHALOM	*Peace* Judges 6:24; Romans 15:33
JUDGE	*Judge* Psalm 7:8; 96:13; 2 Timothy 4:8
JEHOVAH-SHAMMAH	*The Lord Is There* Ezekiel 48:35; Matthew 28:20
DELIVERER	*Deliverer* Psalm 18:2; 144:2

REDEEMER	*Redeemer (One who sets free by buying back, by paying a price)* Job 19:25; Psalm 19:14; Isaiah 54:5
SHIELD	*Shield, Protector, Covering* Psalm 3:3; 18:30
WORD	*Logos* John 1:1; Revelation 19:13
MIGHTY GOD	*Mighty God, Hero* Psalm 24:8; Isaiah 9:6; Luke 9:43
ELOHIM	*Strength or Power* Isaiah 12:2; 26:4; Psalm 18:1-2; Habakkuk 3:19
JEHOVAH-ROHI	*Shepherd, Caretaker, Overseer* Psalm 23; 95:7; 100:3; Isaiah 40:11
FATHER	*Father* 2 Samuel 7:14-15; Psalm 68:5; Isaiah 63:16; 64:8; Matthew 5:16; Luke 6:36
JEHOVAH-NISSI	*Banner* Exodus 17:15

As you study the character of God and experience his power at work in your life, your trust in him will increase. Each life experience in which we encounter the power of God leads to new hope and strengthens our desire to wait on the promises of God. This hope and patience is necessary for walking through times of questionable circumstances. This kind of faith justifies us and causes us to experience peace. Consider Romans 5:1-5 KJV:

> Therefore being justified by faith, we have peace with God through our Lord Jesus Christ: by whom also we have access by faith into this grace wherein we stand, and rejoice in hope of the glory of God. And not only so, but we glory in tribulations also: knowing that tribulation worketh patience; and

patience, experience; and experience, hope: And hope maketh not ashamed; because the love of God is shed abroad in our hearts by the Holy Ghost which is given unto us.

We will be compensated for having hope and confidence in God as we endure circumstances that we cannot rationalize. "Cast not away therefore your confidence, which hath great recompense of reward. For ye have need of patience, that, after ye have done the will of God, ye might receive the promise" (Hebrews 10:35-36 KJV). It is not enough to simply obey God or go through the motions of obedience without confidence in Him. Do not be guilty of obeying God out of fear and failing to act in faith, for this kind of obedience will yield nothing.

SEEK GOD FOR ANSWERS

When your life has been turned upside down, it is reasonable that you will have some questions for God. It is okay to ask God questions, in fact, God told us, through the prophet Jeremiah, "Call to Me and I will answer you and show you great and mighty things, fenced in and hidden, which you do not know (do not distinguish and recognize, have knowledge of and understand)" (Jeremiah 33:3 AMP). If you need wisdom, if you want to know what God wants you to do—ask him and he will gladly tell you. He will not resent your asking.[3] God does not want you to be baffled, bewildered, or confused. He desires to share with you his will for your life.

The love of God is so great that he died for us—his friends.[4] A friendship is a pleasurable relationship. Friends share intimacy and communicate with one another; they share secrets and details about their plans for the future. Such is our relationship with God. Since he calls us his friends, when we commune with him, he will share with us his plans for our lives. The deep, inner meaning of the Word of God is shared with those who are in covenant relationship with him. "Henceforth I call you not servants; for the servant knoweth not what his lord doeth: but I have called you friends; for all things that I have heard of my Father I have made known unto you" (John 15:15 KJV).

TRUST GOD

Your ability to trust God depends heavily on your understanding of God's love for you. Children have confidence in their parents because they know that they are loved by them. Children feel loved, safe, and secure when they are with their parents. This is representative of the relationship that we should have with our heavenly Father. God loves us with an everlasting love, and with loving-kindness, he draws us unto himself.[5] God's love and faithfulness toward us cause us to trust him. God's love for us is very powerful; "God shows and clearly proves His [own] love for us by the fact that while we were still sinners, Christ (the Messiah, the Anointed One) died for us" (Romans 5:8 AMP). "In this is love, not that we loved God, but that He loved us and sent His Son to be the propitiation (the atoning sacrifice) for our sins" (1 John 4:10 AMP).

In response to God's love, "Lean on, trust in, and be confident in the Lord with all your heart and mind and do not rely on your own insight or understanding. In all your ways know, recognize, and acknowledge Him, and He will direct and make straight and plain your paths" (Proverbs 3:5-6 AMP). "For God is not the author of confusion, but of peace" (1 Corinthians 14:33 KJV).

LEARN TO DEPEND ON GOD

When we experience trouble or are just uncomfortable with our circumstances, we usually look for someone to lean on. We will often call a friend to vent and seek advice instead of seeking peace from God and allowing him to direct us. When you are going through your wilderness experience and rebuilding the walls of your life, well-meaning family members and friends may offer their assistance, whether in word or deed. However, this may be a season when you must rely only on God and allow him to direct you. This exercise will cause your faith to increase as you are learning to depend on God. "It is better to trust in the Lord than to put confidence in man" (Psalm 118:8 KJV). "For there is a way that seemeth right unto a man, but the end thereof are the ways of death" (Proverbs 14:12 KJV). The easy way out of any situation may end in destruction.

Follow God's plan exactly; do not take any shortcuts. The process must include prayer and persistence. Commit your way unto God and practice resting and waiting on Him. Depending on God is not an automatic response. As infants, we are conditioned to cry for help, and someone will respond by meeting our needs. As children, when we fall and scrape our knees, our caretakers pick us up and comfort us. Therefore, as adults, when we hurt, are in emotional distress, or experience painful circumstances, we want and expect someone to make us feel better. However, "As for God, his way is perfect, the word of the Lord is tried; he is a buckler to all them that trust in him" (2 Samuel 22:31 KJV).

As we learn to depend on God, we must rehearse Scriptures like Psalm 37:7. We should mediate on them, pray them several times a day, and read them aloud so that we may hear them. Psalm 37:7 says, "Be still and rest in the Lord; wait for Him and patiently lean yourself upon Him" (AMP). Picture yourself leaning on a strong rock—something large and strong enough to hold the weight of your burdens. Do not simply see yourself sitting on that rock; rather, see yourself leaning and resting on that rock. According to Deuteronomy 32:4 (AMP), "He is the Rock, His work is perfect." David sang a song of praise in 2 Samuel 22:2-3: "The Lord is my rock, my fortress, and my savior; my God is my rock, in whom I find protection. He is my shield, the power that saves me, and my place of safety. He is my refuge, my savior, the one who saves me from violence" (NLT).

BROKEN TO BECOME A BELLWETHER

Usually when we think of sheep, we think of them as followers; but a shepherd often designates a sheep to lead the flock. The lead sheep is called the bellwether. The shepherd hangs a bell around its neck so that it can be heard by the other sheep as it moves. The word *wether* means a male sheep that has been castrated (emasculated, deprived of strength, or weakened).[6] The bellwether is a leader; he takes initiative and establishes trends. In order for God to use us as bellwethers (lead sheep), he must first castrate us (cause us to be broken) so that we can be used by Him. We have to be broken to be designated lead sheep by the shepherd. According to Psalm 51:17 (KJV), "The sacrifices of God are a broken spirit: a broken and a contrite heart, O God thou wilt not despise." "The Lord is nigh unto them that are of a broken heart; and saveth such as be of a contrite spirit" (Psalm 34:18 KJV). For Jesus said, "My grace is sufficient for thee; my strength is made perfect in weakness" (2 Corinthians 12:9 KJV).

The old English word *foment* means to promote development; to cause growth; to stir up or call to action. *Foment* traces back to the Latin word *fovere,* which means to heat; to cause stimulation by heat; to irritate. In the early 1600s, doctors would advise patients to foment their injuries (apply heat) to stimulate the area.[7] There are times when God has to foment us. He has to promote growth in us by turning up the heat on our areas of brokenness. You might be thinking: "Haven't I suffered enough? I'm tired of going through this; when am I going to come out?" Do not despise the chastening of God nor faint when you are rebuked, for it is a necessary aspect of training.[8] This is why Joseph had such a long preparation season.

Joseph was approximately seventeen years old when God gave him the dream that he would become a powerful leader. However, he patiently endured more than a decade of testy situations before his dream was realized. Joseph was broken by his pitfall, and the heat was turned up through his experiences in Potiphar's house and prison. These experiences caused growth in Joseph; they stimulated wisdom, knowledge, and skills in him that would prepare him for his purpose.⁹

GOD WILL FULFILL HIS PROMISE TO RESTORE

As demonstrated in the book of Ezra, God will fulfill his promise to restore. Through every experience, God proves himself faithful to his people. God gives us instructions and strategies to succeed. After the Jews were released from exile by King Cyrus, they were instructed to rebuild the temple (place of worship), build reform (return to their covenant obligation of restoring the worship), and to rebuild the wall (reestablish boundaries and protection from the enemy invasions).¹⁰ In Ezra chapter four, the adversaries of the people of God attempted to hinder the work of rebuilding the temple. However, as was prophesied by Haggai and Zechariah, the temple was completed.¹¹ God has promised a complete restoration! As we rebuild our walls, God will rebuild our hearts so that we will truly obey and worship Him. Therefore, when our hearts are turned toward God, he completely restores us.

When life does not make sense, we still have a responsibility to trust God and conduct ourselves in a way that reflects our faith in Him.

A PRAYER FOR YOU

For this reason [seeing the greatness of this plan by which you are built together in Christ], I bow my knees before the Father of our Lord Jesus Christ, for Whom every family in heaven and on earth is named [that Father from Whom all fatherhood takes its title and derives its name]. May He grant you out of the rich treasury of His glory to be strengthened and reinforced with mighty power in the inner man by the [Holy] Spirit [Himself dwelling in your innermost being and personality]. May Christ through your faith [actually] dwell (settle down, abide, make His permanent home) in your hearts! May you be rooted deep in love and founded securely on love, that you may have power and be strong to apprehend and grasp with all the saints [God's devoted people, the experience of that love], what is the breadth and length and height and depth [of it]; [That you may really come] to know [practically, through experience for yourselves], the love of Christ, which far surpasses mere knowledge [without experience]; that you may be filled [through all your being] unto all the fullness of God [may have the riches measure of the divine Presence, and become a body wholly filled and flooded with God Himself]! Now unto Him Who, by (in consequence of) the [action of His] power that is at work within us, is able to [carry out His purpose and] do superabundantly, far over and above all that we [dare] ask or think [infinitely beyond our highest prayers, desires, thoughts, hopes, or dreams]—to Him be glory in the church and in Christ Jesus throughout all generations forever and ever. Amen (so be it) (Ephesians 3:14-21 AMP).

CHAPTER 2

MY PAIN, HIS PURPOSE

God has a plan and a purpose for every man and woman he creates, including those who may not walk out his purpose for their lives. Every great man and woman of God has suffered during their journey to accomplish the will of God. It is important that we know God's purpose for our lives, that we may understand the reason for our affliction. "We are assured and know that [God being a partner in their labor] all things work together and are [fitting into a plan] for good to and for those who love God and are called according to [His] design and purpose" [Roman 8:28(AMP)].

DEVELOP THE CHARACTER OF GOD

All things work together to produce in us the character of God necessary to accomplish his purpose. "Dear brothers and sisters, when troubles come your way, consider it an opportunity for great joy. For you know that when your faith is tested, your endurance has a chance to grow. So let it grow, for when your endurance is fully developed, you will be perfect and complete, needing nothing." (James 1:2-4 NLT). When you are experiencing trouble, use it as an opportunity to grow. Seek God for what you need to learn from the experience and how it can shape your character. Your character is made up of the innate traits, moral quality, integrity, and features that you possess. Do not begrudge your suffering; it may be God's way of preparing you for your purpose! Your suffering may even be God's way of getting you to take a different position on some matters so that your life lines up with his will for you. See it as God's way of doing damage control.

Perhaps you have gotten yourself into a mess and your trouble is a result of your own indiscretions. God loves you too much, and your purpose is too important for Him to allow you to remain in your condition. The Amplified version of Hebrews 12:8 says that you are illegitimate offspring and not a true child of God if you are left without correction and training. During my childhood I had chores; it is the same in the kingdom of God. All children of God have chores; if you are a member of the household of faith, you have some chores. So God has to prepare you for your kingdom responsibilities. As a child you received your allowance once your chores were done; so it is in the kingdom—you receive a reward. "For the time being no discipline brings joy, but seems grievous and painful; but afterwards it yields a peaceable fruit of righteousness to those who have been trained by it [a harvest of fruit which consists in righteousness—in conformity to God's will in purpose, thought, and action, resulting in right living and right standing with God]" (Hebrews 12:11 AMP).

ACCOMPLISHING THE WILL OF GOD

All things also work together to accomplish the will of God in our lives. The book of Esther is a good example of the will of God being accomplished through one's pain. Esther thought that her position as queen was a result of her circumstances; she did not realize at her commencement as queen that God was setting her up for her purpose. God placed her in the position as queen so that she would be in the right place at the right time. God knew before she was conceived that the time would come when she would be used as a catalyst for the deliverance of the Jews. In retrospect, the death of her parents and her being raised by Mordecai were all part of God's plan for positioning her for purpose. When she was grieving the loss of her parents, she probably wondered why she had to suffer; why she had to go through that painful experience. Esther's life is a lesson of understanding the process of fulfilling one's assignment.

Joseph had to go through a lengthy season of pain for the purpose of rescuing the household of his father Jacob (Israel), during the time of famine. Joseph was thrown into a pit by his brothers. He was sold to the Egyptians as a servant of Potiphar. He was falsely accused and imprisoned. All of these circumstances worked together for his good, because they placed him in the right place at the right time. Joseph transitioned from being a slave, to a prisoner, to an administrator (governor).[1] God had promised to build a nation from the family of Abraham, Isaac, and Jacob, despite all of the trouble that this family would experience.[2] God used a famine to reunite the family of Jacob. Joseph rescued the Israelites by inviting them to move to Egypt to escape the famine. The Israelites eventually became a great nation, as promised by God. The salvation of Israel was critical to the birth of Jesus because he is a descendent of Judah, Israel's son.[3] All of this was the purpose for Joseph's pain.

UNDERSTANDING YOUR PURPOSE

What is your purpose? What is God preparing you for? What does God want to accomplish through you? Reflect on some events in your life that have led to the place where you are now. Seek God for answers to these critical questions. "He is a rewarder of them that diligently seek Him (Hebrews 11:6 KJV). God has been preparing you for your purpose since your birth. Every detail of your life has been orchestrated for your purpose. Even those things that seem insignificant have been planned by God—for example, your birth order. If you are the oldest child or the only child, you probably have leadership qualities that have been developing since you were young. As the oldest child, you probably learned to be responsible for others (management). As the only child, you probably learned how to stand alone on issues (forerunner, initiator).

Your educational and employment experiences can be used by God to prepare you for your purpose. Even if you have experienced failure in these areas, it can be used by God. If you did not do well in school, maybe you learned to glean knowledge and wisdom from others. That taught you to establish strong relationships (discipleship). Consider the many ways God can use your experiences.

As we are learning to walk by faith and not by sight through our painful experiences, we must know that suffering is necessary. It is God's way of developing his character within us. Allow God to develop within you the fruit of the Spirit: love, joy, peace, long-suffering, gentleness, faith, meekness, and temperance.[4] Developing the characteristics of God is critical to carrying out his will. If you are having difficulty bearing your cross, consider that Jesus was able to endure the pain of the cross because he understood his purpose.[5]

CHAPTER 3

IT DID NOT COME TO KILL YOU: IT'S ONLY A TEST!

A test is a procedure to detect the presence or absence of something. God uses tests as tools to measure our spiritual growth and maturity. The outcome or result of our testing demonstrates to God and to others the measure of our faith, maturity, growth, and love for Him. All of these measures are judged not on how tough we are, but how well we submit to and lean on God. We must trust in the Lord with all of our heart and lean not on our own understanding, but to acknowledge God and allow Him to direct our paths.[1] God allows and guides us through critical evaluations or examinations to prove us. Therefore, he establishes the truth of who we are in him by argument or evidence. Through these tests, he demonstrates the validity and sincerity of our relationship with him.

There are times in life when you should welcome a test, especially when you are looking to be elevated to the next level in ministry, your career, your relationships, or your social status. When you understand the purpose for a test, your attitude toward that test is not negative, and you will trust God to direct you through it. If you could visualize the end result of your test, it would be easier to endure. When you can see the light at the end of the tunnel, you will know that there is an expected end to your ordeal. When you know that the purpose of the test is not to kill you but to act as the threshold to your next level, you will be encouraged to complete your test.

Tests are inevitable; it is certain that in life there will be tests. The word of God expresses clearly that we should not be shocked by tests, we should not act like it is a strange thing to have trouble in our lives. "Beloved, do not be amazed and bewildered at the fiery ordeal which is taking place to test your quality, as though something strange (unusual and alien to you and your position) were befalling you. But insofar as you are sharing Christ's sufferings, rejoice, so that when His glory [full of radiance and splendor] is revealed, you may also rejoice with triumph [exultantly]" (1 Peter 4:12-13 AMP).

Do not begrudge your time of testing: "Blessed (happy, to be envied) is the man who is patient under trial and stands up under temptation, for when he has stood the test and been approved, he will receive [the victor's] crown of life which God has promised to those who love Him" (James 1:12 AMP). Now that we know that all of us will experience some seasons of testing, we must prepare for the tests.

Test Preparation

Preparing for a test is a strategic process. By communing with God, studying the Word of God, and living according to his Word, you can be prepared for any test, whether it is a planned exam or a pop quiz.

Commune with God: If we are in regular communication with God through the reading of his word, through prayer, and listening to the word of God, when tragedy strikes, we will be equipped to hear and discern the voice of God when he says: It's only a test; this did not come to kill you! I encourage you to listen with expectancy to what the Lord says, for he speaks peace to his people.[2] As mentioned in the previous chapter, it is important to trust God rather than man and to allow him to be your confidant and guide you through your trials. However, if you have not practiced communicating with God, you may feel compelled to turn to other people for their opinions. It will be difficult to hear God in the midst of your test when chaos is all around you. Prepare for your test—practice listening to God, now! "It is better to trust in the Lord than to put confidence in man" (Psalm 118:8 KJV).

It is critical that we hear the word of God, for it increases our faith in him and helps us pass our tests. "Listen (consent and submit) to the words of the wise, and apply your mind to my knowledge; for it will be pleasant if you keep them in your mind [believing them]; your lips will be accustomed to [confessing] them. So that your trust (belief, reliance, support, and confidence) may be in the Lord, I have made known these things to you today" (Proverbs 22:17-19 AMP). Time spent listening to the word of God is an investment in faith because faith comes by hearing the word of God.[3] Strength and courage are a byproduct of the faith that we gain by listening to the word of God. As our faith is stirred by the word of God, he fortifies us and prepares us for our tests.

Study the Word of the Lord: We are to follow the instructions that the Apostle Paul gave Timothy: "Study and be eager and do your utmost to present yourself to God approved (tested by trial), a workman who has no cause to be ashamed, correctly analyzing and accurately dividing (rightly handling and skillfully teaching) the Word of Truth" (2 Timothy 2:15 AMP). The only way to pass the test is to be prepared for it. We must have enough of the Word of God in us to be able to recall it at test time. You will not know how to act or what to do during your test if you have not studied. Imagine your test as an internship or practicum. In many professions, before you can do a practicum or internship, you must first do some observation hours. These observation hours allow you to see how others conduct themselves or practice their profession. Well, studying the Word of

God allows us to see how others in the body of Christ conducted themselves during their tests.

Psalm 1:2-3 teaches that a righteous man delights in and desires the instructions of God, so he ponders and studies them day and night. This daily meditation on the word of God causes him to be as strong as a tree firmly planted near streams of water, *ready to bring forth* fruit in its season. This tree is able to withstand gusty winds and treacherous storms. Its leaves will not fade or wither, and in the midst of the worst circumstances, this tree will come to maturity and bear fruit. Trees receive nutrients from soil and water. When a tree is planted near a stream, its roots are able to grow deeper, which allows the tree to become stronger. If we can be compared to trees, then passing a test requires maturity that only comes by hanging out near the streams. We receive our nutrients from the word of God. Meditate on the word of God, so that you may be ready for your test. Sometimes God allows us to be tested that he might make us know that all we really need is him. "And he humbled thee, and suffered thee to hunger, and fed thee with manna, which thou knewest not, neither did thy fathers know; that he might make thee know that man doth not live by bread only, but by every word that proceedeth out of the mouth of the Lord doth man live" (Deuteronomy 8:3 KJV).

Walk According to the Word of the Lord: When we live according to God's word, he illuminates or gives clarity to our lives. As a protector of our lives, he defends us from attacks. Even when God allows Satan to test us, we should know that he won't be allowed to try us beyond God's limits. As a light, the Holy Spirit will direct our paths. We cannot go wrong when we follow the path that God directs us through, but this requires obedience. "For the Lord God is a Sun and a Shield; the Lord bestows [present] grace and favor and [future] glory (honor, splendor, and heavenly bliss)! No good thing will He withhold from those who walk uprightly" (Psalm 84:11 (AMP). If we fail to obey God, we follow our own path, which prolongs our test.

If you are walking along the path that God established for you, when a test or storm comes, you will be able to stand. Even in the midst of confusion you won't faint, because you will know that you are safe in the arms of the Lord. There is safety in the foundation of living for God. "Anyone who listens to my teachings and follows it is wise, like a person who builds a house on solid rock. Though the rain comes in torrents and the floodwaters rise and the winds beat against that house, it won't collapse because it is built on bedrock. But anyone who hears my teaching and doesn't obey it is foolish, like a person who builds a house on sand. When the rains and floods come and the winds beat against that house, it will collapse with a mighty crash" (Matthew 7:24-27 (NLT).

THE RIGHTEOUSNESS OF GOD REVEALED

Job lost everything in order for God to demonstrate his validity as a perfect, upright and God-fearing man. God proved to Satan that Job's relationship with him was real, and that it was established on the love of God not on the blessings of God.[4] Job was an upright man who feared God. As Satan was walking about seeking someone to devour, God gave him permission to test Job. Job's restoration occurred after he came to the conclusion that all of his suffering was a part of God's purpose. Job had to accept his suffering as the will of God even when he did not fully understand God's plan. This was the proof that Job actually was what he was described to be in chapter one, "a righteous man."

Our tests come to humble us and to prove us, to show what is in our minds and our hearts, to reveal whether we would keep God's commandments or not.[5] We must "walk in the spirit and . . . not fulfill the lust of the flesh" (Galatians 5:16 KJV). When we are going through a test, our flesh desires to know every detail about what God is doing. However, it is not necessary for us to know or understand every detail. True righteousness is reflected when we can accept the will of God even when we do not understand it. Like Abraham, our trust in God is counted as righteousness.[6]

THE BLESSING AFTER THE TESTING

In the end, Job was restored with twice as much as he lost.[7] "God blesses those who patiently endure testing and temptation. Afterward they will receive the crown of the life that God has promised to those who love him" (James 1:12 NLT). God can keep us so well in our wilderness that there will be no evidence of our struggles. Deuteronomy 8:4 tells us that despite a forty-year journey, the Israelites' clothes and shoes did not wear out. Even in the midst of his testing, Job knew his test score; he knew the result of his test even before he completed it. "But he knoweth the way that I take: when he hath tried me, I shall come forth as gold" (Job 23:10 (KJV). Job knew that he would be justified by his faith in God and proven pure and innocent.

Transitioning to the next level would not be a possibility without the shed blood of Jesus. God would have no need or desire to use us in his service if he saw us as we are. Instead, he sees us through the blood of Jesus. In spite of everything that we go through, we must thank Jesus for making it possible for us to be tested and for demonstrating how to go through the test and pass it. It should be our prayer that we honor God with the way we bear our own crosses. We have the assurance from Jesus himself, who said, "These things I have spoken unto you, that in me ye might have peace. In the world ye shall have tribulation: but be of good cheer; I have overcome the world" (John 16:33 KJV).

CHAPTER 4

RELATIONSHIP MATTERS

A relationship with God is the cornerstone of faith. Everything that you have read thus far is moot for individuals without a covenant relationship with God. Walking by faith requires uncompromising righteousness. The just—the uncompromisingly righteous—live by faith, according to their convictions, their belief in the promises of God.[1] When Abraham believed God for the promise of a son, the Bible says that his faith was counted unto him as righteousness.[2] David defeated his enemies because of his relationship with God. King Saul became jealous of David and wanted to kill him. However, he was afraid of David because he knew that David's righteousness had earned him the favor and protection of God.[3]

The spiritual maturity that is required to walk by faith is only possible when one is in a covenant relationship with God. A branch not connected to the vine will dehydrate, wither, and die. We must live in connection with God, and his word must live within us. Just as a branch cannot bear fruit without being connected to the vine, we cannot be sustained and succeed without being in relationship with God.[4] It is God who gives us power to overcome mountains and valleys. Just as a branch is nurtured because it is connected to the vine, we are nurtured by our source. Our creator feeds us the nutrients that are required to build the strength necessary to walk the path of faith.

God expects the sacrifice of righteousness and a holy life. Paul, inspired by God, urged the Romans: "I beseech you therefore, brethren, by the mercies of God, that ye present your bodies a living sacrifice, holy, acceptable unto God which is your reasonable service" (Romans 12:1 KJV). It is a reasonable expectation that we would seek to obey the commandments of God and strive for perfection. It is our responsibility to present our lives to God daily and to ask him to reveal our sins to us that we may repent. This causes us to view sin as God does. We should have disdain for sin and feel repulsed by it just as he does. As we take on the attributes of Jesus Christ through our righteous living, we begin to hate sin. This brings about our repentance from unrighteousness.

Our relationship with God is based on our ability to *trust* Him, our willingness to *submit* to Him, and our allowing Him to *position* us. Trusting God means that we rely on his character, his distinctive qualities, moral excellence, and reputation. Trust is a critical element in our ability to submit. We do not submit to people that we do not trust. We learn to trust the character of God by getting to know him through studying his Word, praying consistently, and hearing his Word.

Submission involves committing to the discretion or decision of another person. To trust God, we must commit to his discretion or to his decisions for our lives. We must trust that God knows what is best for us and yield to his decisions. As we surrender to the discretion of God, we may find ourselves in places and positions that are uncomfortable, painful, frightening, and do not make sense to us. Therefore, we must take on the mind of Christ so that we may have peace even in the midst of storms.[5] The following scripture tells the story of Jesus' authority over storms.

As evening came, Jesus said to his disciples, "Let's cross to the other side of the lake." So they took Jesus in the boat and started out, leaving the crowds behind (although other boats followed). But soon a fierce storm came up. High waves were breaking into the boat and it began to fill with water. Jesus was sleeping at the back of the boat with his head on a cushion. The disciples woke him up, shouting, "Teacher, don't you care that we are going to drown?" When Jesus woke up, he rebuked the wind and said to the waves, "Silence! Be still!" Suddenly the wind stopped, and there was a ***great calm. And he asked*** them, "Why are you afraid? Do you still have no faith?" The disciples were absolutely terrified. "Who is this man?" they asked each other. "Even the wind and the waves obey him!" (Mark 4:35 NLT).

STORMS ALLOW US TO EXPERIENCE THE DEMONSTRATION OF GOD'S POWER

In Mark chapter 4, Jesus *instructs* the disciples regarding the kingdom of God through the use of parables. However, to demonstrate the power of the kingdom of God, he allowed the disciples to experience a storm. It was important for the disciples to be recipients of the miracles of Jesus as well as witnesses to them. The storm was used as a teaching tool. As you are going through your storm, consider it a direct and intentional teaching tool used by God to demonstrate the power of his kingdom in your life. God can speak to your storm with the same power he displayed on that boat. So, *why are you so afraid?* Is it because you do not trust or have faith in God? Has he not demonstrated in previous storms that he can bring you out? Submit to the demonstration of God's power.

Do Not Rely on Self-Confidence to Get You through Your Storm

"True righteousness before God is linked to genuine faith in God. A proud person relies on self, power, position and accomplishment; a righteous person relies on the Lord."[6] "I will listen [with expectancy] to what God the Lord will say, for He will speak peace to His people, to His saints (those who are in right standing with Him)—but let them not turn again to [self-confident] folly" (Psalm 85:8 AMP). If you will confidently lay your frustrations, anxieties, etc., at the feet of the Lord and wait patiently for an answer, God will speak to you concerning your situation. He will speak peace to your storm and speak direction to you.

Prayer Is Critical to Staying in Position

We should always pray and not faint.[7] To faint is to be weak, to fail in heart, to lose courage, or to be weary.[8] If we fail to pray, we will become weak and lack direction from the Holy Spirit. If we fail to have fellowship and intimacy with God, we will be double-minded, unstable, and unsure of our path (confused).[9] Prayer will help you to do the right thing as you are waiting for the storm to clear. Prayer will help you to wait patiently upon the Lord. It will help you walk in peace and self-control. It is possible to be in the midst of a storm without the manifestation of anxiety and panic. We can find rest in God by answering his invitation when he says: "Come unto me, all ye that labor and are heavy laden, and I will give you rest" (Matthew 11:28 KJV).

We must spend time in the presence of God so that when our storms come, we will not be discouraged or dismantled (removed from our high place) by them. In Psalm 18:32-33 (KJV), David (in the presence of God) encouraged himself by saying, "It is God that girdeth me with strength and maketh my way perfect. He maketh my feet like hinds' feet and setteth me upon my high places."

When we are in the presence of God, he speaks to us. It is in his secret place where we receive shelter from our storms. Do not allow yourself to be caught in a storm without the shelter of a relationship with God.

CHAPTER 5

DEVELOPING A LISTENING EAR

It is important to listen to the voice of God as we walk through our valley experiences. In Psalm 25:14, the Word of God tells us that friendship with the Lord is reserved for those who fear him. It is with them that he shares the secrets of his covenant. This is revealed also in Jeremiah 33:3, where the Lord said, "Call to Me and I will answer you and show you great and mighty things, fenced in and hidden, which you do not know (do not distinguish and recognize, have knowledge of and understand)" (Jeremiah 33:3 AMP).

Many times, God uses our valley experiences to draw us unto himself. He desires for us to call upon him and seek to know his will concerning our tests. He says, "Call unto me" shout, cry, announce boldly your request, seek redemption, seek communication with me, address me by name and transfer control to me. For "I will answer you"—I have a solution to your problem, and I will reply. I desire to "show you great and mighty things"—I will permit you to see those things that were previously hidden from you. I will reveal my purpose for your pain, that you may be encouraged in battle to walk according to faith and not flesh.

DISCERN THE VOICE OF GOD—DO NOT BE DIVERTED BY DISTRACTIONS

Fasting and praying are crucial elements to discerning the voice of God as he responds to your cry. Turning over your plate and depriving your flesh of the satiation and pleasure of food and other indulgences will cause you to hear God's voice so clearly that you cannot miss him. Hearing God's voice has to be intentional; we must seek to hear his voice by eliminating distractions. To hear the voice of God, we must spend quality time in his presence so that we can become familiar with his character and his voice. When fasting, it is critical that you abstain from all forms of media and electronics, including social media, television, music, email, text messaging, and telephone. During a fast, God may tell you to eliminate Christian television and music so that you can receive a pure, unfiltered message directly from him. As with any conversation, you cannot clearly hear when you are talking or when there is noise in the background.

Walking by faith requires us to follow the voice of God as our guide. Imagine being blind and allowing someone to lead you through a place that you have never been simply by using verbal instructions—no physical guidance, no guide dog, and no guide stick. First, you would have to be familiar with the voice of your guide to know whose commands to follow. Second, you would have to learn to ignore other outside stimuli to avoid distraction. Third, you would have to learn to understand the timing of your guide.

We, like sheep, should only follow the voice of the shepherd who feeds us.[1] We are fed from the hand of our shepherd, therefore we recognize his voice. It would be foolish for us to knowingly ignore the voice of the one who feeds us and instead follow a shepherd who does not possess the ability to take care of us. According to Jeremiah 33:1-3 (KJV), before the Lord declared his promise to answer and deliver the captive Israelites, he announced himself: "Thus saith the Lord the maker thereof, the Lord that formed it, to establish it; the Lord is his name." He made sure that they knew and understood that he had the power to perform the promise by referencing his role in the creation. He wanted them to know that if he could speak a word and create the heavens and the earth; surely he could deliver them from captivity. This should be a reminder for us to trust God as the "author and finisher of our faith" (Hebrews 12:2 KJV). He created us, so he can keep us!

A relationship with God is the foundation for walking by faith. Relationships require time and attention. If you were in a relationship with someone who invited you over for dinner and during the entire meal your date watched television, answered the telephone, sent text messages, and checked his or her email, you would think that this person was rude, disrespectful, and not really interested in you. This is how many of us treat God. We say that we love God and that we have a relationship with him, but we never spend quality time with him.

In the Bible, Daniel was known as a prophet who heard God's voice clearly and accurately interpreted dreams. Daniel lived a consecrated life, a life dedicated to sacrifice. In Daniel chapter 1, he refused to eat the meat and drink the wine given to him by King Nebuchadnezzar. He consumed only vegetables and water; this was an example of Daniel's commitment to God. As a result of his sacrifice and commitment, "Daniel had understanding in all visions and dreams" (Daniel 1:17 KJV).

God has called us to be *ready listeners*. "Understand [this], my beloved brethren, let every man be quick to hear [a ready listener], slow to speak" (James 1:19 AMP). We must carefully walk the path of God and not turn from our course or purpose by the distractions Satan uses. Ignore the noise! Do not allow any noise to distract your attention from the presence of God. Only in the presence of God will we find the works of his hand. When we are drawn away from God, we become confused and begin to have conflicting emotions and motives; we become double-minded and unstable.[2] This inner conflict will take us off the path of faith.

DISCERN THE TIMING

Listening requires an understanding of timing. As we listen to God (our guide), we come to know and understand the timing or pace of his speech. We must follow the rate of his movement and learn to walk in like manner with him. God knows his plan as it relates to his purpose. It is our responsibility to keep up with his pace. We must move at the speed of God and according to his direction. We must be willing to shift, pivot, and change course in an instant. Genesis 22:1-14 recounts an example of Abraham's obedience and ability to hear and appropriately respond to the voice of God. God sought to prove Abraham's faithfulness. He commanded that Abraham offer his promised son Isaac as a sacrifice. In his obedience, Abraham took Isaac to Mount Moriah, built an altar there, and stacked the wood. He bound Isaac with rope and laid him upon the wood. Abraham lifted the knife to slay Isaac and the "angel of the Lord called unto him out of heaven, and said, Abraham . . . Lay not thine hand upon the lad, neither do thou anything unto him" (Genesis 22:11-12 KJV). Abraham looked up and saw a ram caught in a bush, and he offered up the ram as a burnt offering unto God. Thank God for Abraham's spirit of discernment. Abraham's ability to hear the voice of God and change course in the timing of God is an example of a listening ear.

We must be careful how we listen, for it will determine our spiritual knowledge.[3] Our spiritual knowledge determines how well we follow God. If we dedicate ourselves to listening to the voice of God, he will give us a vision of the end. He will share with us the hidden treasure of his purpose for our pain.

In Romans 8:14, Paul instructs the Christians on living in the Spirit: "For as many as are led by the Spirit of God, they are the sons of God" (KJV). To discern the times and seasons, we must be led by the Spirit of God. A person who is able to understand timing is wise because he/she listens for instructions from God. According to Proverbs 8:33-34, we must hear the instructions of

God and obey them. We are blessed with the wisdom to respond appropriately to our circumstances when we hear and watch daily. We must habitually listen for God and watch for signs from God as indications of the times and the seasons. When we watch for God, we see him in all kinds of situations. From birth to death, we can see God orchestrating our lives and causing all things to work together for our good. God will give us signs of the times and instruct us on how to respond to each situation.

"The children of Issachar . . . were men that had understanding of the times, to know what Israel ought to do" (1 Chronicles 12:32 KJV). They were men of excellence, bravery, and wisdom who excelled in military strategy.[4] God blessed the tribe of Issachar to recognize, discern, and know how to respond to seasons, opportunities, and appointed times. When Jacob, Issachar's father, blessed him, he prophesied to Issachar that he was a strong donkey who was able to bear heavy weight, resting between the sheepfold who would recognize a good land in which to settle down and submit himself to work in that land.[5] This prophecy was a forecast of the legacy of the tribe of Issachar. When Jacob blessed Issachar, he activated the anointing to understand times and seasons and the wisdom to know how to respond. We must seek God for this level of understanding and wisdom so that we will walk by faith in synch with God's timing. To develop a listening ear, we must follow the teacher, Jesus. Jesus knew the importance of watching his Father so he would know what to do. In John 5:19, Jesus taught that children can do nothing on their own. Children only do what they see their father do, and the father takes pleasure in telling his children what he is doing, so that they can do likewise. God desires that we have the information that we need to succeed in our adversities, therefore he rewards our efforts as we ask him to guide us through this walk of faith.

CHAPTER 6

A STRENGTH EXCHANGE: OUT OF CONTROL AND LOVING IT!!!

Submitting to the authority of God requires us to be out of control. We must allow God to regulate our behavior, our emotions, and our attitude regarding our circumstances. Submission to God is a reflection of faith in him. Faith produces obedience and a readiness to yield to God's authority. Unfortunately, there are times when we are prepared to yield to God only after we have tried to change our circumstances and alter our path, to no avail. This failure is just the preparation we need to lift our hands in submission to God. As we are walking through difficult situations, we must commit ourselves to God's care with the knowledge that he will give us the strength to endure every attack. "Many are the afflictions of the righteous; but the Lord delivereth him out of them all" (Psalms 34:19 KJV).

God's grace is more valuable than any of our efforts and sufficient to care for us better than we could care for ourselves. The Apostle Paul had a condition that he described as a thorn in his flesh. In acceptance of his own weakness, Paul begged God three times to remove this painful condition from him. In 2

Corinthians 12:9-10 (AMP), Paul describes God's response and his own acceptance of it:

> But He said to me, My grace (My favor and loving-kindness and mercy) is enough for you (sufficient against any danger and enables you to bear the trouble manfully); for My strength and power are made perfect (fulfilled and completed) and show themselves most effective in [your] weakness. Therefore, I will all the more gladly glory in my weakness and infirmities, that the strength and power of Christ (the Messiah) may rest (yes, may pitch a tent over and dwell) upon me! So for the sake of Christ, I am well pleased and take pleasure in infirmities, insults, hardships, persecutions, perplexities and distresses; for when I am weak [in human strength], then am I [truly] strong (able, powerful in divine strength).

God did not remove Paul's painful, irritating, and possibly embarrassing situation. Instead, he told Paul that his grace—his divine influence upon Paul's heart and his divine influence reflected in Paul's life—was enough to defend him during his time of weakness. Paul recognized that he was strong and able to succeed in accomplishing the will of God and completing his assignment while experiencing affliction when he exchanged his weakness for God's strength.

GOD IS IN CONTROL!

Yielding to God's control requires that we allow ourselves to be restrained by God. This means that he has a direct influence over our lives: He controls our actions, attitudes, thoughts, and conversations. Our ability to endure testing rests in the strength of God, not our own. Our effectiveness is determined by how well we submit to the power of God. When Abraham and Sarah attempted to control their circumstances, Ishmael was conceived. They considered their own weaknesses. Instead of relying on the strength of God, Sarah reflected on her barrenness and Abraham considered his aging body. Due to Abraham's and Sarah's failure to submit to God's strength, they yielded to the fear produced by waiting and devised their own plan to conceive, later regretted by Sarah.[1] By relying on our own strength instead of God's, we create struggles and make life more difficult. We must act according to the instructions of Paul: "But I say, walk and live [habitually] in the Holy Spirit [responsive to and controlled by and guided by the Spirit]; then you will certainly not gratify the cravings and desires of the flesh (of human nature without God)" (Galatians 5:16 AMP).

After Sarah and Abraham yielded to the temptation of time and used Hagar to conceive them a son, God returned to visit them. Again, he promised that they would have a son. Sarah laughed in disbelief, but later "the Lord visited Sarah as he had said, and the Lord did unto Sarah as he had spoken. For Sarah conceived, and bare Abraham a son in his old age, at the set time of which God had spoken to him" (Genesis 21:1-2 KJV). "Is anything too hard for the Lord" (Genesis 18:14 KJV)? No. God proved that he was still in control.

TRUST IS A PREREQUISITE TO RECEIVING GOD'S STRENGTH

If we are going to receive anything from God, we must learn to trust him: "Trust (lean on, rely on, and be confident) in the Lord and do good; so shall you dwell in the land and feed surely on His faithfulness, and truly you shall be fed" (Psalm 37:3 AMP). We walk in God's strength when we dwell in his presence. "Blessed (happy, fortunate, to be envied) are those who dwell in Your house and Your presence: they will be singing Your praises all the day long" (Psalm

84:4 AMP). Our trust in God establishes a strong, fortified place in us; it encourages and strengthens us. "The way of the Lord is strength and stronghold to the upright, but it is destruction to the workers of iniquity" (Proverbs 10:29 AMP).

RESTING IN THE HAND OF GOD

We can rely on God because he gives us the ability and power to endure any storm if we only trust Him. "The Lord will give [unyielding and impenetrable] strength to His people; the Lord will bless His people with peace" (Psalm 29:11 AMP). God will lead us into a state of calm and quiet, especially freedom from disturbing thoughts and emotions. This is the sweet peace that God has promised those who walk upright before him. "You will guard him and keep him in perfect and constant peace whose mind [both its inclination and its character] is stayed on You, because he commits himself to You, leans on You, and hopes confidently in You" (Isaiah 26:3 AMP). When we rest and confide in the strength of God, we shall have peace. Do not trust your own strength or even consider your weaknesses, faults, limitations, or failings; simply trust the strength of God.

It is okay to feel out of control and helpless, just know that God's grace is effective during such times! The power of God rests upon us when we are out of control. As we walk by faith through life's storms, we must exchange our weakness for God's strength. "Have you not known? Have you not heard? The everlasting God, the Lord, the Creator of the ends of the earth does not faint or grow weary; there is no searching of His understanding. He gives power to the faint and weary, and to him who has no might he increases strength [causing it to multiply and making it to abound]" (Isaiah 40:28-29 AMP). There is power in experiencing a *strength exchange* with God!

When we are accustomed to being in control of our circumstances and using our resources and abilities to get us out of arduous situations, it is difficult to be in a position in which our wherewithal is insufficient and we must rely on someone else. This is particularly true for those of us upon whom everyone else seems to rely for solutions and strength. We are resourceful, knowledgeable, confident, and strong—and yet we find ourselves in an insurmountable predicament in which the tables have turned and we cannot help ourselves or anyone else. We have never been here before and we are uncomfortable, embarrassed, and even ashamed. Initially we fight it; we try every trick that we know. Only after every failed attempt do we surrender and allow God to have control. When we experience the care of God and come to understand that he can take better care of us than we can care for ourselves, we can begin to appreciate being out of control. It is then that we realize that we were never truly in control after all. God has always taken care of us, and it was he who blessed us with the resources on which we previously relied.

CHAPTER 7

WALKING BY FAITH TO YOUR EXPECTED END

There are times when God uses unpleasant and uncomfortable circumstances to prepare us for our purpose, but he gives us a map for walking through these circumstances to get to our destination. "For I know the thoughts and plans that I have for you, says the Lord, thoughts and plans for welfare and peace and not for evil, to give you hope in your final outcome" (Jeremiah 29:11 AMP).

The book of Jeremiah recounts the life of the Jews as they were in exile, and it tells of God's plan to release them. The Jews had been warned many times to turn from their lives of sin, disobedience, and destruction, but they were so caught up in drunkenness that they began to self-destruct. They were the people of his covenant, therefore, God would not allow them to be destroyed. Instead, God had to circumcise their hearts. He had to cause their repentance, so that their hearts would turn toward him. God wanted his people to live lives that represented him inwardly and outwardly.

"God is not a man, that he should lie; neither the son of man, that he should repent: hath he said, and shall he not do it? Or hath he spoken, and shall he not make it good?" (Numbers 23:19 KJV). God would not abandon his principle of reward and discipline even for people he loved and with whom he had covenant. To bring them to an expected (right, proper, promised, necessary) end, God had to have them carried away captive (they were carried out of their sin).

Of course, they could not see God working in their situation. They were focused on the circumstances of captivity and their captor, King Nebuchadnezzar. Jeremiah spoke with the voice of God that King Nebuchadnezzar was simply a servant, an agent or instrument of God. God used King Nebuchadnezzar to accomplish his will of taking the Israelites out of their sin, so that in the end they would receive the promise of God.

Jeremiah wrote a letter to the Jews in captivity, informing them that they would be in Babylon for seventy long years. He instructed them to settle down, to build homes and plant crops, to get married and have babies. Most of all, he reminded them to be patient; to exercise composure, even in exile. Keep in mind that these were the same people who were drunk in Jerusalem—so composure was not their strength.

Exile for them did not mean enslavement or imprisonment. It meant displacement or resettlement in an unknown land—not only to punish them but to chasten them. During this time, Babylon was transforming from an aging city to a more prosperous one. The city grew and underwent major cosmetic improvements, including stunning new buildings. God encouraged his people through Jeremiah: If they would be *faithful,* God would cause them to prosper in exile. If they would be obedient to pray for Babylon, they would experience the grace of God while they were there. The seventy years that they would spend in Babylon represented the fullness or fulfillment of God's plan. This is a lesson for believers today: Every season has value. We must study to embrace every season of our lives and seek understanding of the value of each of them.

There is value in experiencing displacement, pain, the wilderness, storms, rejection, and sickness. These experiences often encourage self-assessment. "Examine, test, and evaluate your own selves to see whether you are holding to your faith and showing the proper fruits of it. Test and prove yourselves [not Christ]. Do you not yourselves realize and know [thoroughly by an ever increasing experience] that Jesus Christ is in you—unless you are [counterfeits] disapproved on trial and rejected?" (2 Corinthians 13:5 AMP). The way you walk through your storm will determine your end; it will show or reveal your fruit. That is the value of the test! The Lord is telling you not to begrudge the tests or storms that you experience. Allow him to complete the work that he has begun in you—God will not change his plan.

GOD WILL NOT CHANGE HIS PLAN

Despite the Jews' feelings of displacement, God did not change his plan for them. His plan for Israel was the same as it is for us today. According to Romans 12:12 (KJV), we are to be "rejoicing in hope, patient in tribulation; continuing instant in prayer." We are to be patient and composed even in our displacement, in our place of discomfort, distress, hurt, and suffering, because it may be according to God's plan.

Your enemy can be used as an agent of God. God can even use your ugly and unpleasant circumstance as the instrument to bring you to a place of promise. King Nebuchadnezzar had his own purpose for carrying the Jews away captive, but God allowed their captivity to be used to chasten them and bring them to a point of repentance. During our times of displacement, we must be willing to step into the unknown and settle there, knowing that God has a plan. This is where faith and trust comes in! Even when you can't see or understand what is going on—will you still trust God?

THE ROAD TO YOUR EXPECTED END

Rejoice in hope. The road to your expected end is *hope* that will cause you to rejoice and will strengthen you to endure your tests. We must rejoice in the hope of the promises God has made. "For all the promises of God in him are yea, and in him Amen, unto the glory of God by us" (2 Corinthians 1:20 KJV). To get to the end of this journey, we must expect that God will fulfill the promises he has made. Expectation breeds excitement, and that leads to the joy of the Lord. Trusting God allows us to rejoice in him as our covering. "Let all those who take refuge and put their trust in You rejoice; let them ever sing and shout for joy, because You make a covering over them and defend them; let those who love Your name be joyful in You and be in high spirits" (Psalm 5:11 AMP).

We should be grateful for our tests and trials because the result of those experiences is the completed development of our character.[1] This kind of victory comes from enduring the tests, seeking God for wisdom about our trials, and from exercising patience as we walk through these experiences to our expected end. By not rushing the process of going through difficulties, we learn to relax and experience peace. A common example might be found in leaving home in plenty of time to get to an appointment and encountering deadlock traffic in your commute. In such a situation, you must decide how to respond. You can choose to be angry, to pound on the steering wheel and grind your teeth—or you can decide to pray, to release it to God and believe that he has a plan beyond what you see. If you choose the first response, you may become tense and rigid; your body will release stress hormones that cause headaches and excess acid that can damage the stomach lining. By choosing the second response, you give yourself the opportunity to grow in hope and mature in wisdom. Which would you rather choose? Take advantage of the process—use the time to pray, listen to worship music and enjoy some time alone with God. The use of these tools will increase peace as you go through the process of any trial.

Regardless of how difficult your test, rejoice in knowing that you are in a privileged place. Through faith, our relationship with God positions us for great favor.[2] Studying the Word of God increases our knowledge of his love for us and causes awareness of his grace toward us. The knowledge of his grace causes us to rejoice in the midst of trials because we know they develop our character and our confidence in God. We shall never be disappointed when we trust in God because faith never fails.

Faith produces strength, incites obedience, and nullifies fear. At approximately ninety years old, through faith, Sarah received the strength to conceive and deliver a son.[3] She did not have a miscarriage, she did not give birth to a stillborn baby, and she did not give birth prematurely. Strength is the power to resist strain or stress, and it produces durability. Strength is the ability to maintain a moral or intellectual position firmly and the power to resist attack. Strength is the capacity for effective action.[4] Through faith, Sarah received power to resist the strain and stress of waiting for the promise of God. God reversed the deterioration of her body caused by the effects of time. Sarah received mental fortitude and spiritual stamina to counter the attack of disbelief. Sarah received wisdom to act effectively by conducting herself in a manner that would produce the desired result.

By faith, Abraham had the courage to obey God when he was instructed to leave his homeland of Ur and travel to an unknown place where God had promised to establish him.[5] By faith, when he was instructed to worship God with the sacrifice of his son, Abraham obeyed God without reluctance and offered Isaac as a sacrifice of worship.[6] By faith, Moses overcame his fear of Pharaoh and led the Hebrew people out of Egypt.[7]

According to the Prophet Isaiah, God desires to comfort the brokenhearted and let them know that the end of their trouble is near. The season of new beginnings and recompense is coming. There will be an exchange of sorrow for joy. We will develop strong and gracefully like oak trees for God's glory and be completely restored and fully established. Even your joy will be restored. You will become a leader in faith. Others will rely on you to teach them the principles of faith. God will ensure your vindication. You will be cleared of shame and dishonor, and you will be rewarded for your faithfulness as a symbol of your covenant relationship with God.[8]

Be patient in affliction. Job is an excellent example of what it means to be patient in affliction. Job suffered sickness and the disaster of losing everything that he possessed. However, he was troubled most because he could not explain his suffering. His circumstances did not make sense to him, yet he continued to trust God, and he waited patiently for his day of deliverance. "So the Lord blessed the latter end of Job more than his beginning: for he had fourteen thousand sheep, and six thousand camels, and a thousand yoke of oxen, and a thousand she asses" (Job 42:12 KJV). Job's patience proved his faith in God, and he received double for his trouble.

Rejoice, because the tests that we endure are not designed to destroy us, but to qualify or approve us. Our adversities are opportunities in disguise. "Be assured and understand that the trial and proving of your faith bring out endurance and steadfastness and patience. But let endurance and steadfastness and patience have full play and do a thorough work, so that you may be [people] perfectly and fully developed [with no defects], lacking in nothing" (James 1:3-4 AMP).

As you are walking through your wilderness toward your expected end, over time you may grow weary and lose sight of promises that God has made. Therefore, you must have a vision of the end. When I was expecting my son, my Lamaze instructor recommended that expectant mothers take an item to the hospital to be used as a focal point during delivery. I chose the outfit that my baby would wear home from the hospital as my focal point. When I arrived at the hospital and was settled in my room, my mother hung the outfit on the wall across from my bed. During most of my labor, I did not pay attention to the outfit, and I actually forgot that it was there. I was in labor about twelve hours. The first eight hours I was uncomfortable but calm. About nine hours into my labor, the spirit of fear came over me and I began to think, *If the pain is this bad now, when it is time to push the pain will be unbearable.* I began to rehearse all of the tools that I received in Lamaze. I gazed across the room and saw my baby's outfit. It reminded me of the purpose for my pain, and I knew that it would soon be over. Focusing on the outfit that my baby would wear home from the hospital brought me comfort and peace as I knew that there was an expected end. Regardless of how long it takes, know that the vision of God's promise shall come to pass. "Then the Lord said to me, 'Write my answer plainly on tablets, so that a runner can carry the correct message to others. This vision is for a future time. It describes the end, and it will be fulfilled. If it seems slow in coming, wait patently, for it will surely take place. It will not be delayed'" (Habakkuk 2:2-3 NLT).

Be faithful in prayer. God is calling us to be dedicated to prayer, so that he may direct our path as we walk to our expected end. "Pray without ceasing" (1 Thessalonians 5:17 KJV). As you walk through your storm, there will be times when you are tempted to give up. In Luke chapter 18, Jesus teaches us why it is important to always pray and not faint. We can learn a lesson from this persistent widow: *Don't give up!*

> One day Jesus told his disciples a story to show that they should always pray and never give up. "There was a judge in a certain city," he said, "who neither feared God nor cared about people. A widow of that city came to him repeatedly, saying 'Give me justice in this dispute with my enemy.' The judge ignored her for a while, but finally he said to himself, 'I don't fear God or care about people, but this woman is driving me crazy. I'm going to see that she gets justice, because she is wearing me out with her constant requests!'" Then the Lord said, "Learn a lesson from this unjust judge. Even he rendered a

just decision in the end. So don't you think God will surely give justice to his chosen people who cry out to him day and night? Will he keep putting them off? I tell you, he will grant justice to them quickly! But when the Son of Man returns, how many will he find on the earth who have faith?" (Luke 18:1-8 NLT)

Reconciliation is a prerequisite for restoration. Prayer is a part of the reconciliation process. "If my people, which are called by my name, shall humble themselves, and pray, and seek my face, and turn from their wicked ways; then will I hear from heaven, and will forgive their sin, and will heal their land" (2 Chronicle 7:14 KJV). God will restore all that you have lost if you will operate according to his plan. Prayer and repentance are catalysts to the promise.

"There is hope in thine end, saith the Lord" (Jeremiah 31:17 KJV). To walk according to God's plan, you must first enter into covenant with him by making him Lord/ruler over your life. Walking by faith to your expected end requires you to remain in the presence of God, patiently wait on Him, and maintain fellowship with Him through prayer, that you may receive your daily instructions.

EMBRACING THE PROCESS

Embrace the process in order to obtain the promise of God. The process is just as important as the promise. Several years ago, I turned on the television and there was a program demonstrating how to make a mosaic. The host described how, over time, she had collected beautiful pieces of fine china. She did not go to garage sales and dime stores. She had visited antique shops and estate sales for months until she had gathered enough china to create the mosaic. The artist collected magnificent cups, plates, and platters from various sets of china, until she was satisfied that she had enough to create a masterpiece.

The first step to creating the mosaic was to break the pieces of china. However, before breaking them, she covered each piece with a cloth to protect it from scattering. The artist did not want the china to be lost in the breaking process. She used a mallet to hammer the china until each item was broken into usable pieces. She carefully laid out each irregularly broken piece on a table and examined them.

As I watched the show, it was difficult to imagine how these oddly shaped, broken pieces of china could be used to create anything of value. The creativity of the artist became evident, as she gracefully and strategically selected and placed each broken piece on the canvas, based on its shape and size. She glued the pieces to the canvas and when it was complete, she sealed the work of art with a grout-like substance and wiped it clean. Finally, the beauty of the mosaic was revealed.

God's process of preparing us for purpose and destiny resembles that of creating a mosaic. First, he calls us to himself and invites us to accept the redemptive blood of Jesus as ransom that we may be forgiven of our sins and escorted into a right relationship with our Creator. Then God covers us before he allows us to be broken—in the time of trouble, he hides us in his shelter; in his secret place, he covers us. God controls the process and the environment: He sets limits and boundaries for how we will be broken. Then the mallet of life's circumstances breaks us in such a way that life is difficult to understand, it does not make sense. We struggle to comprehend why painful events have taken place and what will become of us. The promises of man are broken, our dreams are shattered, and we question God: "How are you going to use this mess? What are you going to do with the fragmented pieces of my broken life? It looks like you have allowed Satan to have his way with me." But just when it looks like the devil has victory over us, God begins the reconstruction process. He lays out the uneven, disjointed pieces of our lives, carefully and strategically selecting each piece. He starts with our character because he knows that the tests of our faith develop patience within us. He calls each shard of us a fruit of his Spirit: love, joy, peace, long-suffering, gentleness, goodness, faith, meekness, and temperance.[9] In this process of being recreated, God teaches us to examine ourselves and begin to see ourselves the way he sees us—the good, the bad and the ugly. Then he gives us the opportunity to repent of everything that does not resemble him. This is the process of the master artist, our Creator. After he strategically places and adheres each piece of our character to the canvas of our being, wasting nothing, he seals us. He seals us in his love, until we learn to love ourselves and appreciate the works of his hands. When we feel inadequate, our confidence will be in him; for the works of his hands are always sufficient. When we look in the mirror, we will see our scars as grout lines. Then God wipes us clean; he wipes away the residue of sin and brokenness. Finally, he places us on a mantel for others to see and admire, for his glory. When God places us on a mantle, he admires our beauty. He appreciates the seams of our once broken pieces; he acknowledges the time spent in his presence during the process of reconfiguration; and he allows us to enjoy the attention of admiration before the next season of tests begins.

Embrace the process of walking by faith to your expected end!

ENDNOTES

INTRODUCTION

1. 2 Corinthians 5:7

CHAPTER ONE
TRUSTING GOD WHEN LIFE DOES NOT MAKE SENSE

1. Psalm 27:5.
2. "trust." The Free Dictionary.http://www.thefreedictionary.com/trust
3. James 1:5
4. John 15:13-15.
5. Jeremiah 31:3.
6. "bellwether." Merriam-Webster Online Dictionary. 2004. http://www.merriam-webster.com/dictonary/bellwether
7. "foment." Merriam-Webster Online Dictionary. 2004. http://www.merriam-webster.com/dictonary/foment
8. Hebrews 12:5-6.
9. Genesis 37-44.
10. *Nelson's New Illustrated Bible Commentary*, 1999 pp 569-570; *Nelson Study Bible* 1988 pp 755-756.
11. Ezra 6:14.

Chapter Two
My Pain, His Purpose

1. Genesis 37-41.
2. Genesis 12:1-3.
3. Genesis 42-45.
4. Galatians 5:22-23.
5. Matthew 20:18-19, 28.

Chapter Three
It Did Not Come to Kill You: It's Only a Test!

1. Proverb 3:5-6.
2. Psalm 85:8.
3. Romans 10:17.
4. Job 1:1, 6-12.
5. Deuteronomy 8:2.
6. Galatians 15:6; Romans 4:3-5.
7. Job 42.

Chapter Four
Relationship Matters

1. Habakkuk 2:4.
2. Genesis 15:6.
3. 1 Samuel 18:12-15.
4. John 15:2-4.
5. Philippians 2:5.
6. *Nelson's New Illustrated Bible Commentary* © 1999 (Habakkuk 2:4).
7. Luke 18:1.
8. *New Strong's Expanded Exhaustive Concordance of the Bible, Red Letter Edition*, Thomas Nelson Publishing, Nashville © 2001 (#1573).
9. Proverbs 3:6.
10. Psalm 91.

CHAPTER FIVE
DEVELOPING A LISTENING EAR

1. John 10:4.
2. James 1:8.
3. Luke 8:18.
4. 1 Chronicles 7:5; Judges 5:15.
5. Genesis 49:14-15.

CHAPTER SIX
A STRENGTH EXCHANGE:
OUT OF CONTROL AND LOVING IT

1. Genesis 16:1-4.

CHAPTER SEVEN
WALKING BY FAITH TO YOUR EXPECTED END

1. James 1:2-5.
2. Romans 5:2-5.
3. Hebrews 11:11.
4. "strength." The Free Dictionary. www.thefreedictionary.com/strength
5. Hebrews 11:8.
6. Hebrews 11:17.
7. Hebrews 11:27.
8. Isaiah 61:1-8.
9. Galatians 5:22-23.

Biography of Christian Martin

Christian Martin is a daughter of God who has overcome many obstacles. She has learned to rely on God when she could have leaned on the support of family and friends. The comfort of God has been her solace during times of discontent. Christian understands the value of difficult circumstances and has taken advantage of her tests. She has used complicated experiences as opportunities to extend her knowledge of the power of God as she draws near to Him.

Christian has a passion for assisting others in their quest to overcome tragedy and loss. She has a ministry of faith that enables her to motivate others to appreciate every day of life as an opportunity to rebuild, regardless of past or current circumstances.

Christian is a visionary who recognizes the gifts and talents of individuals and encourages them to seek God and rely on him to reveal his plan for their lives. She motivates individuals to walk step by step into the plan and promises of God.

CPSIA information can be obtained at www.ICGtesting.com
Printed in the USA
BVOW060131240512

290944BV00001B/87/P